# GRANDMA MARGIE TALES OF THE CHILDREN OF ISRAEL CROSS THE RED SEA

Written by renowned author and award winning film maker Dr. K.T. Zulkowski

Published by Mz. Kim Productions

4263 Tierra Rejada Rd #151

Moorpark, CA 93021

www.mzkimproductions.com

ISBN: 978-1-962106-24-5

Printed in United States of America

First Printing: November 2023

Date of Copyright: July 5,2023

For permissions, please contact: Mz. Kim Productions

4263 Tierra Rejada Rd #151

Moorpark, CA 93021

www.mzkimproductions.com

mzkimproductions@gmail.com

# Dedication

I dedicate this book to all the children who have a curiosity for the wonders of the Bible and a desire to learn about the incredible stories of faith and miracles. May this book inspire you to trust in God's plan for your own life and to always remember His love and faithfulness. May you find joy in discovering the power of faith and the miracles that await those who believe.

May you find comfort in the timeless lessons and teachings found within the pages of the Bible, and may they guide you in times of doubt and uncertainty. May this book serve as a reminder that no matter how big or small your faith may be, God can work miracles in your life. May you be encouraged to approach each day with a childlike wonder and a steadfast belief in the power of prayer. May you learn from the examples of the faithful men and women who came before us, and may their stories inspire you to persevere in your own journey of faith. May you be reminded that even in the midst of challenges and trials, God is always with you, ready to work miracles in your life. May you be filled with hope and a renewed sense of awe as you discover the incredible wonders of the Bible. Finally, may this book deepen your love for God and His Word, and may it draw you closer to Him as you embark on this journey of faith and miracles.

This book is also dedicated to the memory of Grandma Margie, whose unwavering faith and love for God continues to inspire us all. Grandma Margie, you were a shining example of a life lived in devotion to the teachings of the Bible. Your kindness, wisdom, and gentle spirit touched the lives of everyone you encountered. We will forever cherish the memories of the countless hours spent reading the Bible together, discussing its lessons, and witnessing your faith in action. Your unwavering belief in God's miracles and your dedication to prayer serve as a constant reminder that miracles are possible for those who believe. Your legacy lives on, and we honor you by sharing the timeless truths contained within this book. May it serve as a testament to your unwavering faith and a source of inspiration for generations to come. Thank you, Grandma Margie, for showing us the power of faith and reminding us that miracles are not just stories from the past but can be experienced in our lives today.

# Educational Value

Overall, this book provides a valuable educational experience by combining

biblical history, moral lessons, and the development of faith. It encourages

children to explore their own beliefs, learn about important biblical events, and

develop a deeper understanding of God's love and protection.

Grandma Margie: Once upon a time, my dear Zipporah and Zion, there was a great adventure that happened long ago. It's a story about the children of Israel and how they crossed the Red Sea.

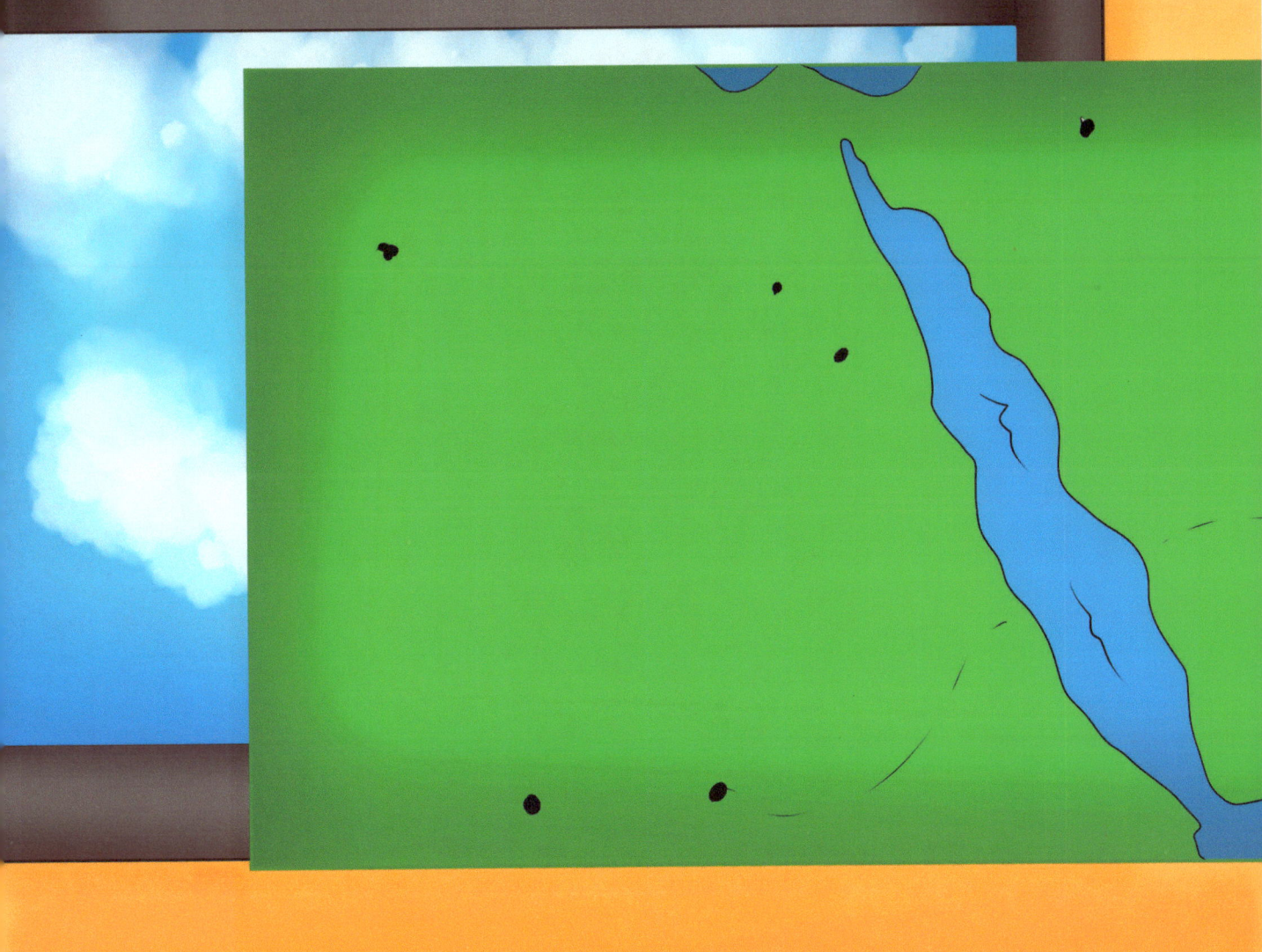

Grandma Margie: Our story begins in Egypt, where the children of Israel were living as slaves. They cried out to God for help, and He heard their prayers. Look, here is Egypt, and this is the Red Sea where the miracle happened!

Grandma Margie: That's Moses, a brave leader chosen by God to free the Israelites. He went to Pharaoh, the king of Egypt, and asked him to let God's people go. But Pharaoh was stubborn and didn't want to listen.

Zipporah: But Pharaoh didn't listen, did he?

Grandma Margie: No, my dear grandson. Pharaoh's heart was hardened, and he refused to set the Israelites free. So, God sent ten plagues to Egypt to show His power. Look at Pharaoh's face, he was not happy!

Zion: Look, Grandma! The Israelites are packing their things!

Grandma Margie: Yes, Zion. After the tenth plague, Pharaoh finally let them go. The Israelites hurriedly gathered their belongings and began their journey to the Promised Land. They were so excited to be free!

Zipporah: Grandma, why did they stop at the Red Sea?

Grandma Margie: Good question sweet Zipporah. God led them to the Red Sea, but they were trapped. In front of them was the sea, and behind them, Pharaoh's army was approaching. They didn't know what to do!

Zion: What did Moses do, Grandma?

Grandma Margie: Moses trusted in God's plan. He raised his staff, and God performed a miracle. The waters of the Red Sea parted, creating a path for the Israelites to cross. Just like this, he raised his staff high!

Grandma Margie: Yes, my dear. The Israelites walked through the sea on dry ground, with walls of water on both sides. It was like walking through a big tunnel made of water!

Grandma Margie: As the last Israelite stepped onto the other side, God commanded Moses to stretch out his hand again. The walls of water came crashing down, swallowing Pharaoh's army. It was a powerful sight, but also a sad one.

Zion: They made it, Grandma!

Grandma Margie: Yes, Zion! The Israelites were filled with joy and gratitude. They praised God for His mighty deliverance and His faithfulness. They danced and sang songs of thanksgiving!

Grandma Margie: They journeyed through the wilderness, guided by God's pillar of cloud by day and pillar of fire by night. They set up camp and learned to trust God for their daily needs. It was a time of testing and growth.

Zion: How long were they in the wilderness, Grandma?

Grandma Margie: They wandered in the wilderness for forty years, my dear Zion. It was a long journey, but God was with them every step of the way. He provided manna from heaven and water from a rock to sustain them.

Zipporah: That's incredible, Grandma!

Grandma Margie: Yes, Zipporah. God's provision was miraculous. He showed His love and care for His people, even in the midst of their challenges. He never left them alone.

Grandma Margie: Yes, Zipporah. God's provision was miraculous. He showed His love and care for His people, even in the midst of their challenges. He never left them alone.

Grandma Margie: It's natural to feel scared when facing something new, my dear Zipporah. The Israelites were unsure of what lay ahead, but God reassured them of His presence and promised to fight for them.

Zion: Did they have to cross another body of water, Grandma?

Grandma Margie: Yes, Zion. Just as God parted the Red Sea, He also parted the waters of the Jordan River. The Israelites crossed on dry ground, entering the Promised Land with great anticipation and gratitude.

Zipporah: What did they do once they were in the Promised Land, Grandma?

Grandma Margie: They settled in the land and began to build their homes and communities. Each tribe received their portion of the land, and they worked together to establish a nation under God's guidance.

Zion: Did they remember what God had done for them, Grandma?

Grandma Margie: It's important to remember God's faithfulness, my dear Zion. The Israelites celebrated festivals and told their children about the miracles God had performed. They knew that their journey was a testament to His love and power.

Grandma Margie: Of course, my dear Zipporah. We can celebrate and remember God's faithfulness in our own lives. We can tell stories and pass down the legacy of His love to future generations.

Zion: Grandma, thank you for telling us this amazing story!

Grandma Margie: You're welcome, my dear Zion. It's a story that reminds us of God's power, love, and faithfulness. May it always inspire and encourage you on your own journey.

Zipporah: We love you, Grandma!

Grandma Margie: I love you too, my sweet Zipporah and Zion. Remember, God is always with you, just as He was with the children of Israel. Trust in Him, and He will guide you through any challenge.

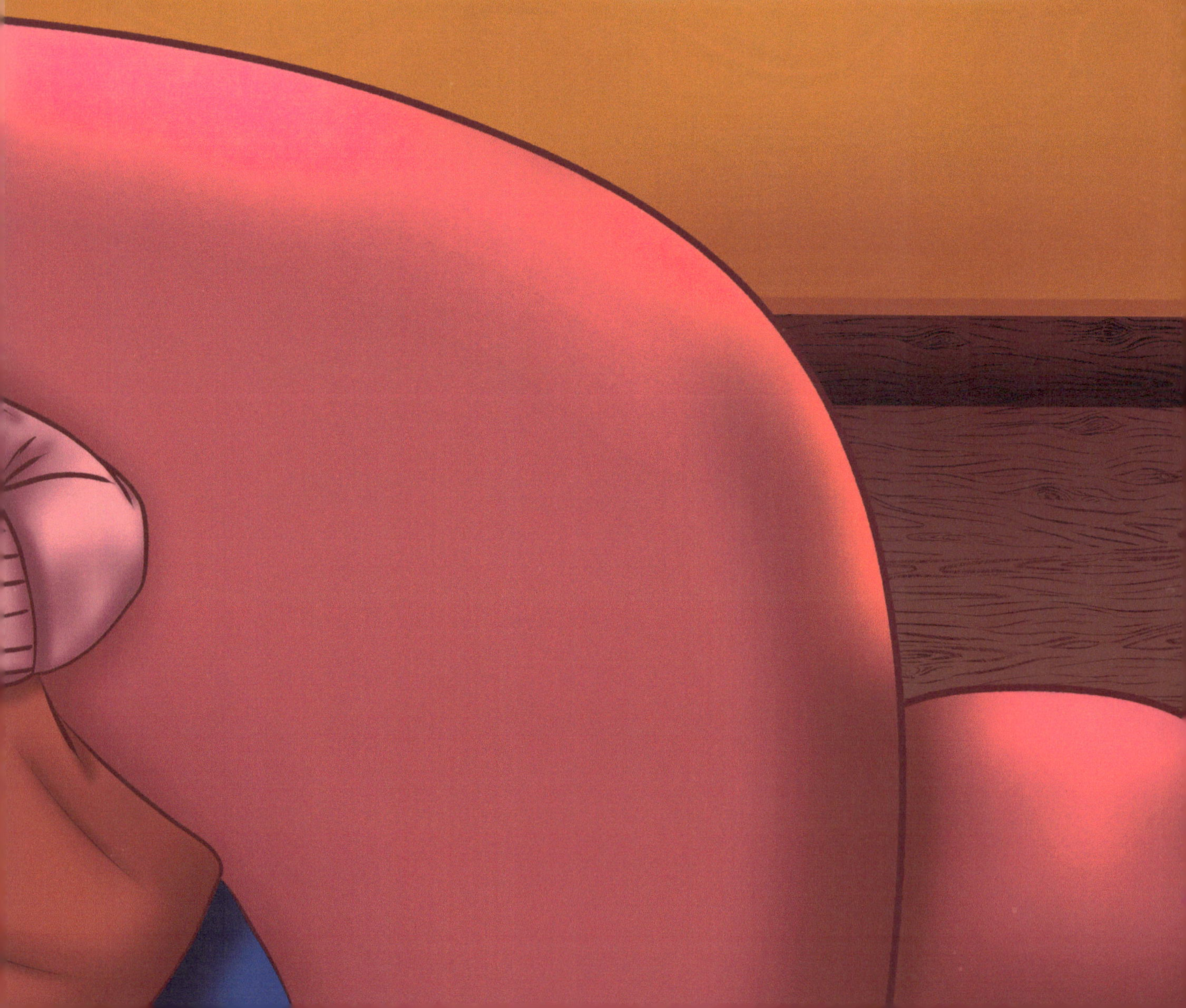

Zion: We will, Grandma. Thank you for teaching us about God's amazing miracles!

Grandma Margie: You're welcome, my dear Zion. Always remember that you are part of a great story, a story of God's love and redemption. Embrace it, and let it shape your lives.

Grandma Margie: And so, my dear Zipporah and Zion, our story comes to an end. But remember, it's not just a story. It's a reminder of God's faithfulness and the incredible journey of the children of Israel. May it always inspire you to trust in Him and walk in His ways.

*The End*

# Author's Note

Dear readers,

Thank you for joining Grandma Margie, Zipporah, and Zion on this incredible adventure through the story of the children of Israel crossing the Red Sea. It has been a joy to bring this tale to life and share it with you.

As you read through the pages of this book, I encourage you to imagine the scenes vividly in your mind. Picture Grandma Margie's warm smile, Zipporah's curious eyes, and Zion's playful energy. Let their expressions and actions guide you through the story, and feel the sense of awe and wonder that filled the air during this miraculous event.

While this book is a work of fiction, it is based on the biblical account of the Israelites' journey. The story of their deliverance from slavery in Egypt and their crossing of the Red Sea is a powerful testament to God's faithfulness and His ability to lead His people through the most challenging circumstances.

I hope that this book not only entertains you but also inspires you to reflect on the themes of trust, faith, and gratitude. Just as the Israelites trusted in God's plan and experienced His miraculous intervention, may we too trust in Him and find comfort in His guidance in our own lives.

Thank you for embarking on this journey with us. May the story of the children of Israel crossing the Red Sea continue to resonate in your hearts and minds.

Warm regards,

Dr. K.T. Zulkowski